# PARES SCALES

### For Individual Study and Like-Instrument Class Instruction

*by* **GABRIEL PARÈS**

**Revised and Edited by Harvey S. Whistler**

## Published for:

Flute or Piccolo . . . . . . . . . . . . . . . . . . . . . Parès-Whistler

Clarinet . . . . . . . . . . . . . . . . . . . . . . . . Parès-Whistler

Oboe . . . . . . . . . . . . . . . . . . . . . . . . . . Parès-Whistler

Bassoon . . . . . . . . . . . . . . . . . . . . . . . . Parès-Whistler

Saxophone . . . . . . . . . . . . . . . . . . . . . . Parès-Whistler

Cornet, Trumpet or Baritone 𝄞 . . . . . . . . . . . Parès-Whistler

French Horn, E♭ Alto or Mellophone . . . . . . . Parès-Whistler

Trombone or Baritone 𝄢 . . . . . . . . . . . . . . . Parès-Whistler

E♭ Bass (Tuba - Sousaphone) . . . . . . . . . . . . . Parès-Whistler

BB♭ Bass (Tuba - Sousaphone) . . . . . . . . . . . . Parès-Whistler

Marimba, Xylophone or Vibes . . . . . . . Parès-Whistler-Jolliff

**For Individual Study and Like-Instrument Class Instruction**
**(Not Playable by Bands or by Mixed-Instruments)**

**RUBANK®**

**HAL•LEONARD® CORPORATION**

7777 W. BLUEMOUND RD. P.O. BOX 13819 MILWAUKEE, WI 53213

Sax. L-112
Oboe L-113

# Key of C Major
## Long Tones to Strengthen Lips

Scale of C

**1**

Also practice holding each tone for EIGHT counts.
When playing long tones, practice (1) ⤙ and (2) ⤙⤚.

981-47

**8**

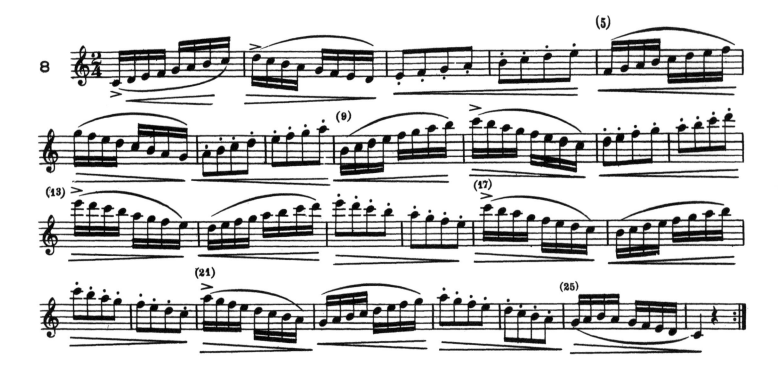

**9**

## Embouchure Studies

Slur as many tones as possible

**10**

Slur as many tones as possible

**11**

# Key of G Major
## Long Tones to Strengthen Lips

Scale of G

**12**

Also practice holding each tone for EIGHT counts.
When playing long tones, practice (1) $\small <$ and (2) $\small <\!>$.

**13**

**14**

**15**

**19**

**20**

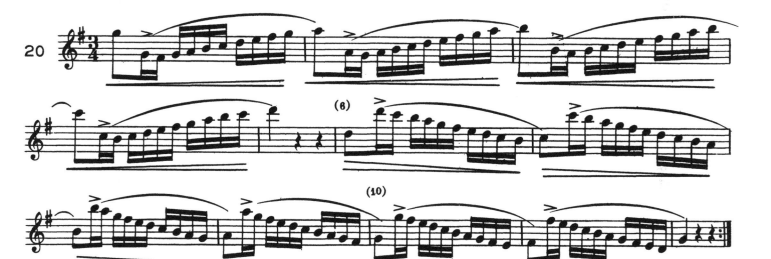

## Embouchure Studies

**Slur as many tones as possible**

**21**

**Slur as many tones as possible**

**22**

# Key of F Major

## Long Tones to Strengthen Lips

**23**

Also practice holding each tone for EIGHT counts.
When playing long tones, practice (1) ⟨ and (2) ⟨ ⟩.

**24**

**25**

**26**

## Embouchure Studies

Slur as many tones as possible

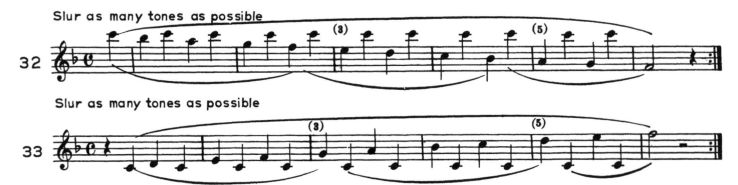

Slur as many tones as possible

# Key of D Major
## Long Tones to Strengthen Lips

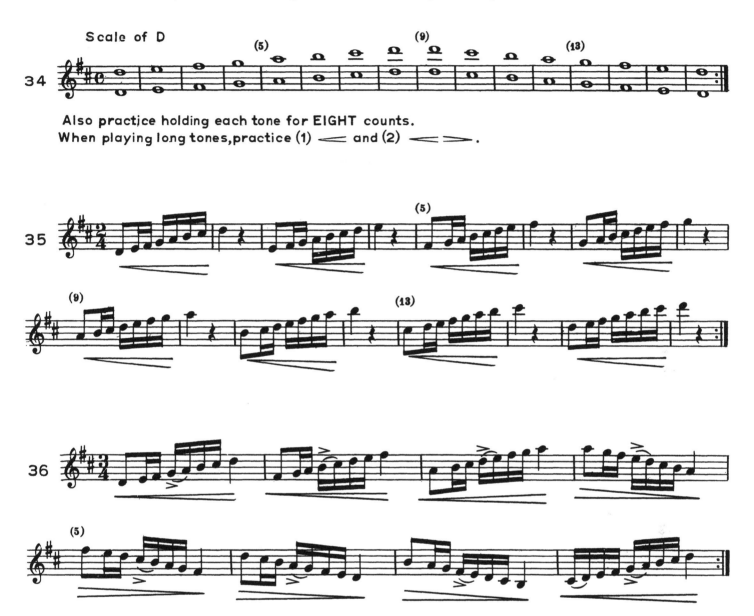

Scale of D

34

Also practice holding each tone for EIGHT counts.
When playing long tones, practice (1) ⊂ and (2) ⊂⊃.

35

36

37

41

42

## Embouchure Studies

Slur as many tones as possible

43

Slur as many tones as possible

44

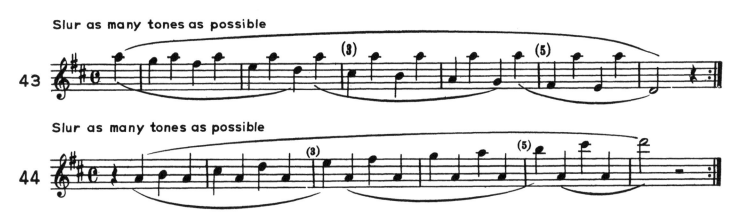

# Key of B♭ Major
## Long Tones to Strengthen Lips

Scale of B♭

45

Also practice holding each tone for EIGHT counts.
When playing long tones, practice (1) ⟨ and (2) ⟨⟩.

46

47

48

49

50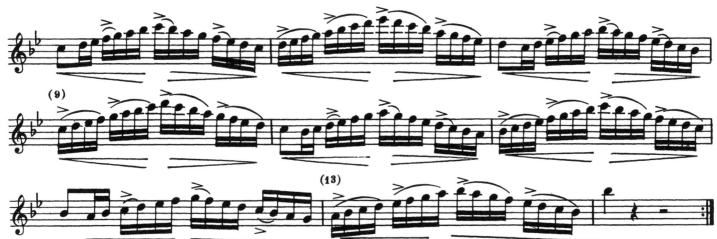

51

## Embouchure Studies

Slur as many tones as possible

Slur as many tones as possible

# Key of A Major
## Long Tones to Strengthen Lips

Also practice holding each tone for EIGHT counts.
When playing long tones, practice (1) $<$ and (2) $<>$.

## Embouchure Studies

Slur as many tones as possible

Slur as many tones as possible

# Key of E♭ Major

## Long Tones to Strengthen Lips

**66** — Scale of E♭

Also practice holding each tone for EIGHT counts.
When playing long tones, practice (1) ⟨ and (2) ⟨ ⟩.

**70**

**71**

**72**

## Embouchure Studies

Slur as many tones as possible

Slur as many tones as possible

# Key of E Major
## Long Tones to Strengthen Lips

**77** Scale of E

Also practice holding each tone for EIGHT counts.
When playing long tones, practice (1) ⊂ and (2) ⊂ ⊃.

**81**

**82**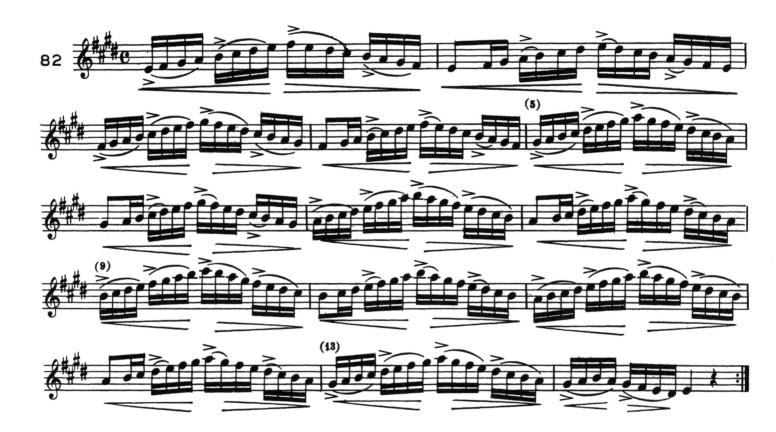

**83**

## Embouchure Studies

Slur as many tones as possible

Slur as many tones as possible

# Key of A♭ Major

## Long Tones to Strengthen Lips

Scale of A♭

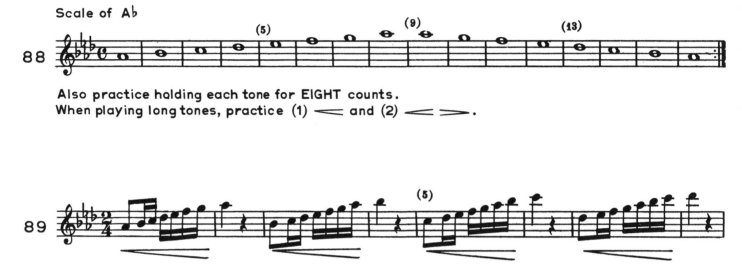

88

Also practice holding each tone for EIGHT counts.
When playing long tones, practice (1) ⟨ and (2) ⟨ ⟩.

89

90

26

981-47

**94**

**95**

## Embouchure Studies

Slur as many tones as possible

**96**

Slur as many tones as possible

**97**

981-47

# Key of A Minor
## (Relative to the Key of C Major)
### Long Tones to Strengthen Lips

Scale of A Harmonic Minor

Scale of A Melodic Minor

Also practice holding each tone for EIGHT counts.
When playing long tones, practice (1) and (2).

## Embouchure Studies

Slur as many tones as possible

Slur as many tones as possible

# Key of E Minor
### (Relative to the Key of G Major)
## Long Tones to Strengthen Lips

Scale of E Harmonic Minor

**104**

Scale of E Melodic Minor

**105**

Also practice holding each tone for EIGHT counts.
When playing long tones, practice (1) ⟨ and (2) ⟨⟩.

**106**

**107**

## Embouchure Studies

Slur as many tones as possible

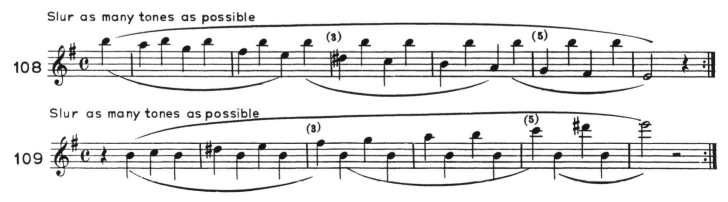

**108**

Slur as many tones as possible

**109**

# Key of D Minor
### (Relative to the Key of F Major)
## Long Tones to Strengthen Lips

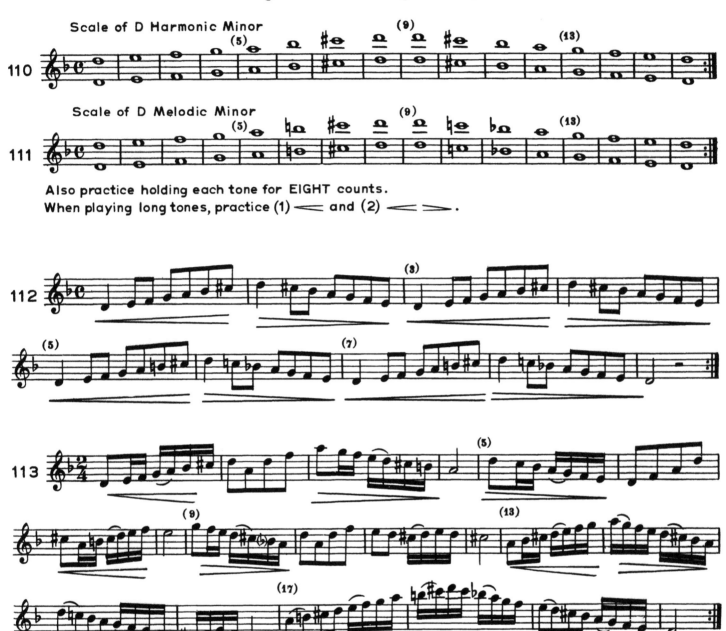

**110** Scale of D Harmonic Minor

**111** Scale of D Melodic Minor

Also practice holding each tone for EIGHT counts.
When playing long tones, practice (1) ⬍ and (2) ◁▷.

**112**

**113**

## Embouchure Studies

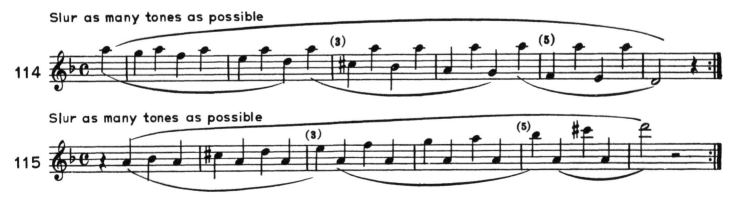

Slur as many tones as possible

**114**

Slur as many tones as possible

**115**

# Key of B Minor

### (Relative to the Key of D Major)

## Long Tones to Strengthen Lips

Scale of B Harmonic Minor

Scale of B Melodic Minor

Also practice holding each tone for EIGHT counts.
When playing long tones, practice (1) $\underset{\phantom{x}}{<}$ and (2) $\underset{\phantom{x}}{<>}$.

## Embouchure Studies

Slur as many tones as possible

Slur as many tones as possible

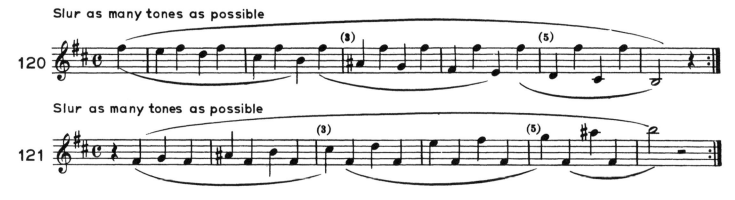

# Key of G Minor
### (Relative to the Key of B♭ Major)
## Long Tones to Strengthen Lips

**Scale of G Harmonic Minor**

**122**

**Scale of G Melodic Minor**

**123**

Also practice holding each tone for EIGHT counts.
When playing long tones, practice (1) ⟨ and (2) ⟨⟩.

**124**

**125**

## Embouchure Studies

**Slur as many tones as possible**

**126**

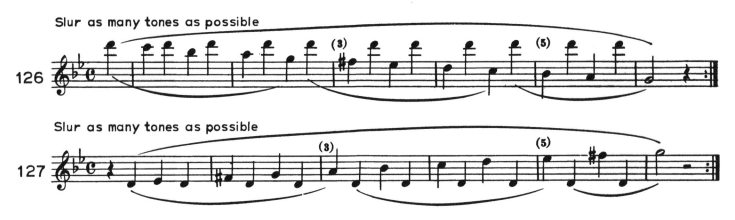

**Slur as many tones as possible**

**127**

# Key of F# Minor
### (Relative to the Key of A Major)
## Long Tones to Strengthen Lips

Scale of F# Harmonic Minor

**128**

Scale of F# Melodic Minor

**129**

Also practice holding each tone for EIGHT counts.
When playing long tones, practice (1) ⟨ and (2) ⟨⟩ .

**130**

**131**

## Embouchure Studies

Slur as many tones as possible

**132**

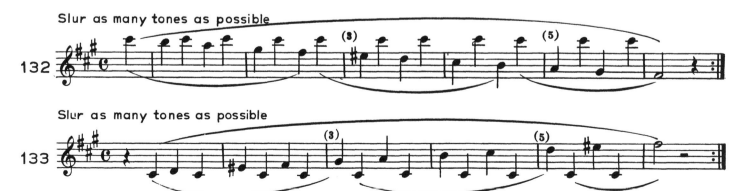

Slur as many tones as possible

**133**

981-47

# Key of C Minor
### (Relative to the Key of E♭ Major)
## Long Tones to Strengthen Lips

**Scale of C Harmonic Minor**

**134**

**Scale of C Melodic Minor**

**135**

Also practice holding each tone for EIGHT counts.
When playing long tones, practice (1) ⟨ and (2) ⟨⟩.

**136**

**137**

## Embouchure Studies

Slur as many tones as possible

**138**

Slur as many tones as possible

**139**

981-47

# Key of C♯ Minor
(Relative to the Key of E Major)
## Long Tones to Strengthen Lips

Scale of C♯ Harmonic Minor

**140**

Scale of C♯ Melodic Minor

**141**

Also practice holding each tone for EIGHT counts.
When playing long tones, practice (1) ⟨ and (2) ⟨ ⟩.

**142**

**143**

## Embouchure Studies

Slur as many tones as possible

**144**

Slur as many tones as possible

**145**

# Key of F Minor
## (Relative to the Key of A♭ Major)
### Long Tones to Strengthen Lips

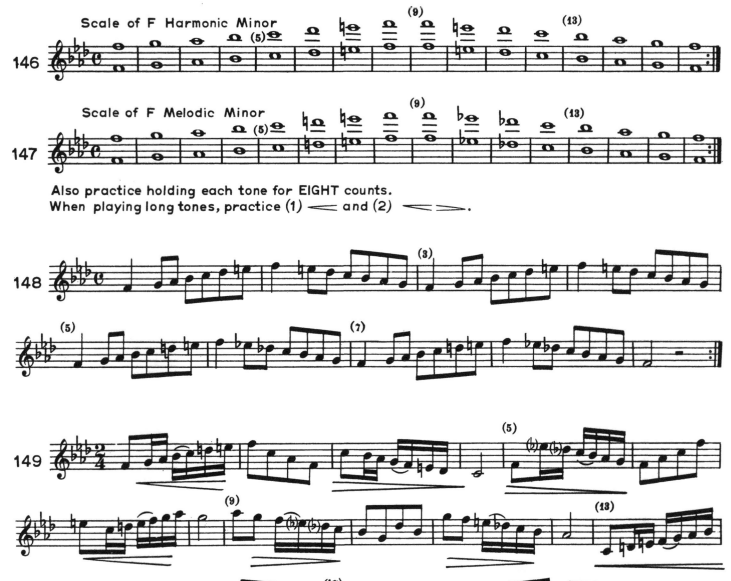

**Scale of F Harmonic Minor** — 146

**Scale of F Melodic Minor** — 147

Also practice holding each tone for EIGHT counts.
When playing long tones, practice (1) $\textit{<}$ and (2) $\textit{<>}$.

148

149

## Embouchure Studies

Slur as many tones as possible

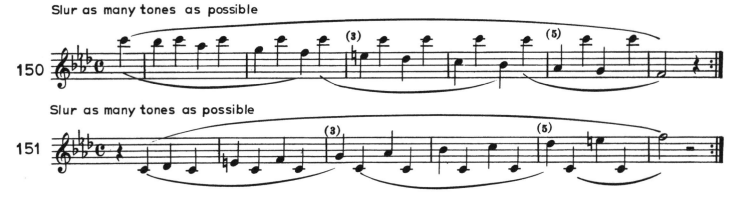

150

Slur as many tones as possible

151

# Major Scales

981-47

# Harmonic Minor Scales

# Melodic Minor Scales

# Arpeggios

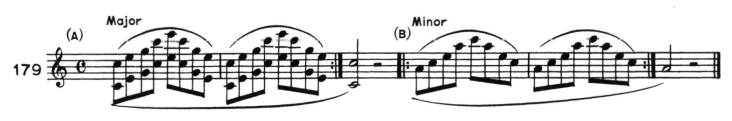

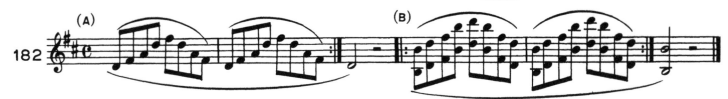

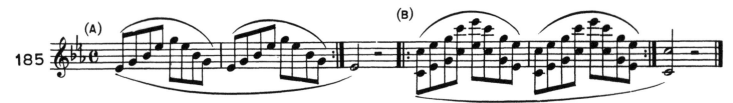

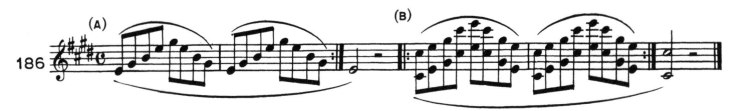

# Chromatic Scales

## Chromatic Scales in Triplets

## Two Octave Chromatic Scales

## Two Octave Chromatic Scales in Triplets

# Basic Exercises to Strengthen Low Tones

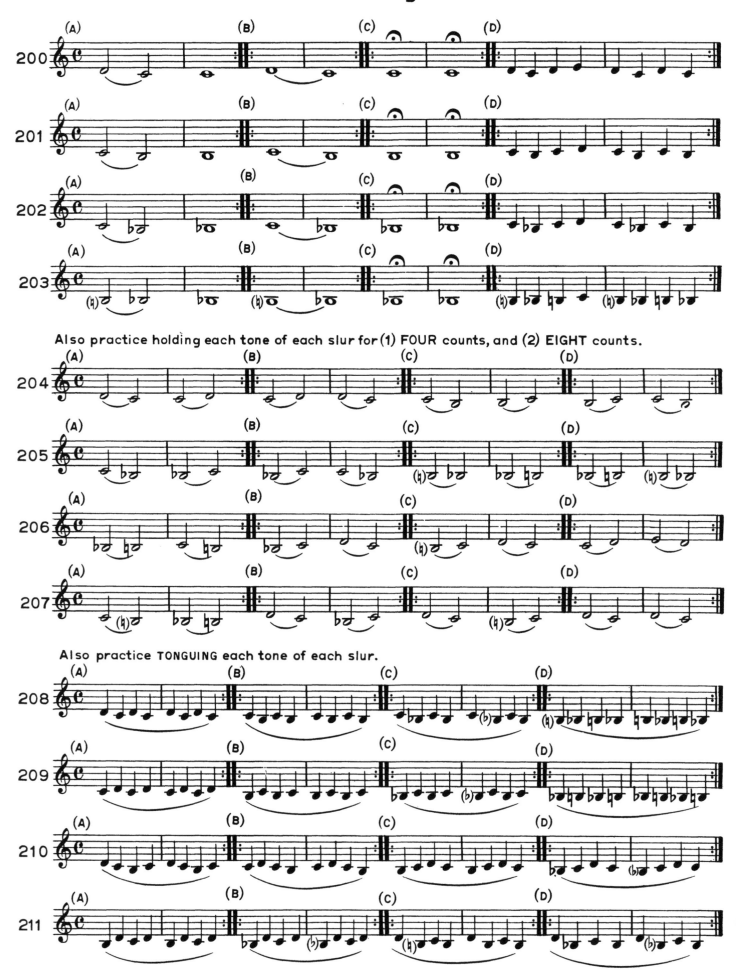

Also practice holding each tone of each slur for (1) FOUR counts, and (2) EIGHT counts.

Also practice TONGUING each tone of each slur.

# Basic Exercises to Strengthen High Tones

## Short Studies in the High Register

(a) Also practice very slowly, holding each tone for (1) FOUR counts, and (2) EIGHT counts.
When playing long tones, practice (1) ⟨⟨ and (2) ⟨⟨⟩⟩ .

(b) Also practice very legato, (1) slurring each two tones, and (2) slurring each four tones.

# Studies in Mechanism

# Scales in Thirds

## Exercise in Sixths

## Combined Thirds and Sixths

## Octave Study